INVASION ALERT!

INVASION OF THE KILLER BEES

DEVON PATRICK

Enslow PUBLISHING

Please visit our website, www.enslow.com. For a free color catalog of all our high-quality books,
call toll free 1-800-398-2504 or fax 1-877-980-4454

Published in 2027 by
Enslow Publishing
2544 Clinton Street
Buffalo, NY 14224

Portions of this work were originally authored by Emily Mahoney and published as *Animal Invaders: Destroying Native Habitats: Attack of the Killer Bees.* All new material in this edition is authored by Devon Patrick.

Cataloging-in-Publication Data
Names: Patrick, Devon.
Title: Invasion of the killer bees / by David and Julie Lavender.
Description: Buffalo, NY : Enslow Publishing, 2027. | Series: Mighty animal migrations | Includes glossary.
Identifiers: ISBN 9781978548398 (pbk.) | ISBN 9781978548404 (library bound) | ISBN 9781978548411 (ebook)
Subjects: LCSH: Africanized honeybee--Juvenile literature. | Dangerous animals--Juvenile literature.
Classification: LCC QL568.A6 D486 2027 | DDC 595.799--dc23

Printed in China

Photos Credits: Cover, p. 1, 11 Scott Bauer, USDA Agricultural Research Service, Bugwood.org; cover, p. 1, 3, 4, 6, 8, 10, 12, 14, 16, 18, 20, 22, 23, 24 (dot pattern) Nurin Nabila A/Shutterstock.com; p. 4, 6, 8, 10, 12, 14, 16, 18, 20 (sidebar frame) HST6/Shutterstock.com; p. 5 Hennie Briedenhann/Shutterstock.com; p. 6 sruilk/Shutterstock.com; p. 7 Henijurnalis/Shutterstock.com; p. 9 Pamela Au/Shutterstock.com; p. 13 aaltair/Shutterstock.com; p. 15 Darios/Shutterstock.com; p. 17 Riko fajar/Shutterstock.com; p. 19 McCann Michelle/Shutterstock.com; p. 20 Omniosis_Productions/Shutterstock.com; p. 21 frantic00/Shutterstock.com

CPSIA compliance information: Batch #QSENS27: For further information, contact Enslow Publishing,
New York, New York, at 1-800-398-2504.

CONTENTS

Words in the glossary appear in **bold** type the first time they are used in the text.

BUSY BEES

Most people have seen plenty of bees. They fly around our backyards and gardens, moving from flower to flower. Some of these helpful critters even make yummy honey. But sometimes they can sting—ouch!

What many people don't know is that a kind of bee called the Africanized honeybee can also be found in your neighborhood, and it might do more harm than just sting. These **aggressive** bees are spreading into parts of the United States. They might take over food and living space from the bees already living there.

STAY ALERT

Africanized honeybees are an invasive species. They can be harmful to native animals and plants when put into a new **habitat**.

There's a reason why their nickname is "killer bees"! Africanized honeybees can cause lots of trouble in North and South America.

TO THE AMERICAS

Before the 1950s, European honeybees were the only type of honeybee in North and South America. However, they did not thrive in the tropical areas near the equator. It was too hot for them.

In 1956, a Brazilian scientist named Warwick Kerr traveled to Africa. He brought some African honeybees back with him. The African bees were used to Brazil's hot weather already! He hoped to **breed** them with European bees to see if their offspring, or young, would make more honey in Brazil's hot climate.

STAY ALERT

Scientists sometimes bring animals to new places on purpose. But even careful plans can go wrong.

Scientists hoped the offspring would have the European bees' gentleness, but it didn't quite work out that way!

ON THE LOOSE

In 1957, some African honeybees escaped from their **quarantines**. At the time, Kerr didn't think it would be a big problem. He believed the African honeybees would die in the new **environment**. Even if they **mated** with the local honeybees, he thought their offspring would be less aggressive.

The African honeybees did mate with the European honeybees, but Kerr was wrong. Their offspring are aggressive and fast-moving. This honeybee **hybrid** became the Africanized honeybees—or killer bees—scientists are worried about today.

STAY ALERT

Of the escaped bees, 26 were queens. Queens are the only bees that mate and lay eggs.

Africanized honeybees can spread quickly. They can travel hundreds of miles each year!

MORE HONEYBEES

Africanized honeybees are slightly smaller than European honeybees, but otherwise look very similar. Both species have brown and yellow stripes. Scientists must do special tests to tell them apart.

However, an easier way to identify them is by their behavior, or how they act. African honeybees are much more **defensive** than European honeybees. If they're worried about an animal near their nest, they are quick to attack. African honeybees also attack in big groups, or swarms. Africanized honeybees have taken on these aggressive **traits**.

STAY ALERT

It takes about three weeks for Africanized honeybee eggs to become full-grown adults.

The populations of Africanized honeybee colonies grow quickly. Each queen may lay as many as 2,000 eggs a day each spring!

SPREADING OUT

Africanized honeybees spread quickly through the warm climates of South America and the southern United States. The weather in these places is similar to what the bees were used to in Africa. Since it's warmer in South America, the bees' population has spread especially fast there.

Swarms of Africanized honeybees may move 60 miles (97 km) or more at a time. They can build their nests in many places. Africanized honeybees are also more **resistant** to other bugs and **diseases** that could harm European honeybees.

STAY ALERT

The first Africanized honeybees spotted in the United States were found in Texas in 1990. Since then, they have moved into more of the southern parts of the country.

Africanized honeybees build smaller hives, so they can start new colonies quickly. European honeybee hives are larger and built to last longer.

KILLER BEES ATTACK

Africanized honeybees have earned the nickname "killer bees." They have the same amount of venom, or poison, in their stingers, but they attack in big groups. A swarm of these invasive bees can sting up to 10 times more than European honeybees! These killer bees can kill both people and large animals.

These invasive bees also harm the environments in which they live. Since they grow and mate at such a fast rate, there often isn't enough food for all of the bees near Africanized honeybee colonies.

STAY ALERT

Africanized honeybees can sense a **threat** to their hive from more than 50 feet (15 m) away! They have also been known to chase these threats over long distances.

Each bee can sting only once before it dies, but a colony of Africanized honeybees will send out many more bees in an attack. The group can sting thousands of times.

BEES MATTER!

Africanized honeybees cause problems, but they're still an important part of their habitat. Without bees, even those that are invasive species, we wouldn't be able to grow many fruits and vegetables! In fact, bees help all kinds of plants grow.

As honeybees search for pollen, they fly between different plants. When they land on a new plant, some of the pollen they've already collected is left behind. The movement of pollen from one plant to another is called cross-pollination. This helps plants grow and make new seeds.

STAY ALERT

Many of the fruits, vegetables, and nuts we eat—such as almonds, apples, carrots, and avocados—need honeybees to help them grow.

The populations of pollinating bugs like bees are in trouble all over the world. Killer bees may be troublemakers, but we still need them!

SLOW THE SPREAD

It's impossible to totally stop the spread of Africanized honeybees. But there might be ways to slow it down.

Beekeepers should continue to raise European honeybees. Over time, European honeybees will breed with the Africanized honeybees, which should lessen their aggressive traits. Also, Africanized honeybees are less likely to build hives in places with lots of European honeybees. If many European honeybee hives already exist in an area, Africanized honeybees are less likely to take over.

STAY ALERT

You can help too! "Bee-proof" your home by keeping food and garbage sealed. Remove or block places in your yard or home where Africanized bees might try to build their hives.

In Central and South America, beekeepers are using killer bees to produce honey just like they hoped to. But they need to be careful—these bees can sting through a beekeeper suit!

HERE TO STAY

Africanized honeybees have settled in the United States. They now live in much of the south, including Arizona, Texas, and Louisiana. They have been found in 13 states and are slowly spreading north.

If you live in a place where Africanized honeybees are, know what to do and what not to do. If you see a beehive, don't bother it. Walk away quickly and tell an adult. If a swarm starts to fly after you, don't swat at the bees. Cover your face and get inside. Tell an adult if you've been stung!

STAY ALERT

Remember, bees that attack are protecting their home and their queen. They are defending their territory.

Africanized honeybees will chase people or animals they think are threats. They'll even wait if you go underwater!

GLOSSARY

aggressive: ready or likely to attack

breed: to mate two animals with desired qualities in order to produce more like them

defensive: having to do with guarding a place and attacking quickly

disease: illness

environment: the conditions that surround a living thing and affect the way it lives

habitat: the natural place where an animal or plant lives

hybrid: something that is made by combining two or more things

mate: to come together to make babies

quarantine: when an animal is kept away from others for a period of time

resistant: able to survive

threat: something likely to cause harm

trait: a feature that is passed on from parents to children

FACT CHECK

1. ________ bees are the only bees that mate and lay eggs.
   a. Aggressive   b. Gentle   c. Queen

2. Africanized and European honeybees look similar except Africanized honeybees are ____________.
   a. smaller   b. larger   c. a different color

3. Africanized honeybees have spread across parts of the ________ United States.
   a. northern   b. southern   c. eastern

Answers: 1. c, 2. a, 3. b

ON THE INTERNET

Bee Facts for Kids

www.pestworldforkids.org/pest-guide/bees/

Learn lots of information about four different types of bees, including killer bees!

Killer Bees for Kids

www.youtube.com/watch?v=XtRINCO5rFs

Watch a short video about Africanized honeybees from Learn Bright to learn more about their diet, behavior, and habitat!

Publisher's note to educators and parents: Our editors have carefully reviewed these websites to ensure that they are suitable for students. Many websites change frequently, however, and we cannot guarantee that a site's future contents will continue to meet our high standards of quality and educational value. Be advised that students should be closely supervised whenever they access the Internet.

INDEX